WIT & WISDOM™

GREAT MINDS® WIT & WISDOM

Grade 8 Module 2:
The Great War

Student Edition

Copyright © 2016 Great Minds®

COPYRIGHT STATEMENT

Published by Great Minds®.

Copyright ©2016 Great Minds®. All rights reserved. No part of this work may be reproduced or used in any form or by any means—graphic, electronic, or mechanical, including photocopying or information storage and retrieval systems—without written permission from the copyright holder.

ISBN: 978-1-68386-050-1

Table of Contents

GRADE 8 MODULE 2

Student Resources

Handout 1A: "The War to End All Wars," Shari Lyn Zuber

Handout 1B: "The Peace President Goes to War," Duane Damon

Handout 1C: Fluency Homework

Handout 2A: Choosing Evidence for Concision and Precision

Handout 5A: Collect Evidence: Two Perspectives

Handout 6A: Military Vocabulary

Handout 7A: Fluency Homework

Handout 8A: Broad Category Organization

Handout 9A: Broad Category Evidence Organization

Handout 11A: Text Analysis

Handout 12A: "Fighting From the Trenches," Kathryn M. Horst

Handout 12B: Fluency Homework

Handout 12C: Multiple Meaning Chart

Handout 13A: Transitions in Writing

Handout 14A: Transitions Experiment

Handout 14B: Descriptive and Sensory Details

Handout 16A: Collect Evidence—Conditions on the Front

Handout 18A: Fluency Homework

Handout 18B: Fluency Homework

Handout 21A: Film Techniques

Handout 21B: Verb Voice T-Chart

Handout 23A: Socratic Seminar Prewriting

Handout 23B: Verb Voice T-Chart

Handout 25A: Film Analysis: "Forgive Me, Comrade"

Handout 27A: Fluency Homework

Handout 29A: Text Analysis

Handout 31A: Frayer Models

Handout 32A: Using an Ellipsis

Handout 34A: End-of-Module Planning Packet

Handout 34B: End-of-Module Exemplar Essay

Handout 34C: Explanatory Writing Checklist

Volume of Reading Reflection Questions

Wit & Wisdom Parent Tip Sheet

Handout 1A: "The War to End All Wars," Shari Lyn Zuber

Directions: Follow along in your copy of the text as you listen to a Read Aloud.

France was humiliated. Within six months, it had been overrun by the newly united Germany in the Franco-Prussian War (1870–1871). In France's Palace of Versailles, Germany officially declared its new empire. This insult was compounded by German demands for a huge war payment and the ceding of France's Alsace-Lorraine region.

Over the previous ten years, Otto von Bismarck, Germany's "Iron Chancellor," had united the Teutonic (Germanic) states by picking fights with other nations and using the conflicts to unify his people. In 1882, to keep France isolated, Germany joined with Austria-Hungary (also known as the Dual Monarchy) and Italy in the Triple Alliance. (During World War I, however, Italy sided against Germany and Austria-Hungary.) By 1907, partially in response to the Triple Alliance, France, Russia, and Great Britain had joined together to form the Triple Entente. These alliances aggravated the already tense situation in Europe by engaging in a competition to see which alliance could accumulate the strongest military force.

A particularly troubled region was the Balkans, an area of southeastern Europe ruled by the Austro-Hungarian and Turkish Ottoman empires. There, a group of ethnic minorities called Slavs longed for their own national identity and began to agitate against domination by these two powers.

In 1912 and 1913, a group of Balkan states defeated Turkey in two short conflicts called the Balkan Wars. One of those states, Serbia (a Slavic state), gained significant territory during the wars. Serbia then called for all Slavs, including those living under the Austro-Hungarian Empire, to unite.

On June 28, 1914, Archduke Francis (or Franz) Ferdinand, the heir to the Austro-Hungarian throne, and his wife, Sophie, were in the empire's Slavic-dominated region of Bosnia. There, Gavrilo Princip, a Serbian nationalist, assassinated them.

Austria-Hungary's harsh ultimatum to Serbia—including the demands to stop anti-Austrian propaganda and to dismiss anti-Austrian government officials—was rejected. The empire, with the unconditional backing of Germany, declared war on Serbia on July 28. In time, the Ottoman Empire (present-day Turkey) and Bulgaria (who had lost territory to Serbia in the Balkan Wars) joined Germany, becoming part of the Central Powers.

Russia came to Serbia's aid. Then Germany declared war on Russia (August 1) and France (August 3). Following Germany's invasion of neutral Belgium on August 4, Great Britain entered the war. Russia, France, and Great Britain then became known as the Allies.

Since the United States traded with both the Allies and the Central Powers, President Woodrow Wilson tried to maintain U.S. neutrality. But to combat a British naval blockade of continental Europe, Germany used a new weapon, the Unterseeboot, or U-boat. While underwater, this submarine was able to launch torpedoes that could sink enemy ships. In

May 1915, the British cruise ship Lusitania, which was carrying American passengers, was sunk. When outraged Americans called for war, President Wilson's strong protests to Germany resulted in a temporary halt to U-boat attacks on passenger vessels and neutral merchant ships, and the United States stayed out of the war.

U.S. neutrality did not last, however. Sabotage orchestrated by the German ambassador in America and the resumption of U-boat activity forced President Wilson to act. On April 6, 1917, the United States entered the conflict, with Wilson declaring that "the world must be made safe for democracy."

When American soldiers landed in Europe in 1917, the Great War had been going on for three years. Germany's 1914 invasion of France through Belgium had stalled outside Paris. Fighting on a second front with Russia further tied up German forces. The arrival of the Americans provided the spirit boost and the manpower that the war-weary Allies needed.

By the end of the year, however, civil unrest in Russia (which brought down the czar and ushered in a Communist government) forced it to withdraw from the war. In March 1918, Russia signed the Treaty of Brest-Litovsk with Germany. With no more battles to distract them in the east, the Germans attempted one final assault in the west on March 21 near the Somme River in France. Over the next few months, the Germans kept striking at the Allied line, knowing that if they did not win soon, they eventually would be outnumbered by the Allies, bolstered by the influx of American soldiers. In June 1918, American commander John "Black Jack" Pershing's forces entered Belleau Wood, a key position on the road to Paris. For twenty days, U.S. Marines struggled through, a yard at a time, and succeeded in taking the wood.

In July 1918, at the Marne River, the tide of battle turned, and the Allies went on the offensive. By the end of September, the German commander advised his government to ask for peace. Throughout the fall of 1918, the Central Powers surrendered one by one. The German leader, Kaiser William (or Wilhelm) II, fled his homeland on November 10. At 11:00 a.m. on November 11, under the Armistice signed outside Paris, the guns on the western front fell silent. What was optimistically referred to as "the war to end all wars" was over. It was time to negotiate a peace.

* -*cede* means "to give up."

* *Sabotage* means "to deliberately destroy or damage property."

* *Armistice* means "a temporary end to fighting."

Handout 1B: "The Peace President Goes to War," Duane Damon

Directions: Follow along in your copy of the text as you listen to a Read Aloud.

On a spring evening in 1917, a former college professor rose to speak in the ornate chamber of the House of Representatives. Seated before him were the assembled members of both houses of Congress. The speaker was Thomas Woodrow Wilson, twenty-eighth president of the United States. For nearly three years, he had struggled to keep the United States at peace. But that night he had come to ask for war.

"It is a fearful thing to lead this great peaceful people into war," Wilson stated solemnly. "But the right is more precious than peace."

The storm of applause that greeted his speech disturbed the troubled president. He knew well the terrible price of warfare. "My message today was a message of death for our young men," he later remarked to an aide. "How strange it seems to applaud that." With those misgivings, Woodrow Wilson led the United States into World War I.

The events that brought the president before Congress that April night began not in the United States but in the tense atmosphere of Europe. There, closely packed nations eyed their neighbors with centuries-old resentments and suspicions. Out of those ancient ill feelings had come the first rumblings of a worldwide conflict.

As the twentieth century opened, the British Empire stood as the mightiest on Earth. Yet Britain was a nervous giant. The rising military and industrial might of Germany caused the British to keep a wary eye on their neighbor across the North Sea. Both countries nursed festering grudges over past clashes and disagreements. Nearby France had its own turbulent history of warring with the Germans.

At the same time, unrest was simmering in Austria-Hungary. Its sprawling empire dominated the peoples of several smaller states, such as Serbia and Bosnia. Many Serbs, Czechs, Poles, and others resented their Austria-Hungarian rulers.

Another factor adding to European tensions was the rise of nationalism, a kind of patriotism gone wild. Nations infected with this dangerous feeling often felt superior to other countries and jealous of their territories.

As fear of war deepened, nations began forming partnerships, or alliances, with other nations. By 1914, Europe was like a cord of dry kindling waiting for a match.

The United States, meanwhile, recently had elected the scholarly, strong-jawed Woodrow Wilson to the presidency. A former university president and New Jersey governor, Wilson had written books and articles on the U.S. government. He had definite ideas on how to do his job. His stubborn devotion to his principles caused some to consider him arrogant and cold. But Wilson had high hopes for the United States. His eloquence and boldness in working toward those ideals made him one of our more influential presidents. Hardly had Wilson settled into the White House when the fateful match was struck in a small province in Austria-Hungary.

On June 28, 1914, Archduke Franz Ferdinand was assassinated in Bosnia by Serbian nationalists. Enraged by the murder of the heir to its throne, Austria-Hungary declared war on Serbia. Within a week, Europe's fragile peace collapsed like a house of cards.

Russia quickly lined up behind Serbia, followed by France and England. Germany joined Austria-Hungary in the opposing camp. As country after country entered the conflict, a British diplomat noted sadly, "The lamps are going out all over Europe."

The United States watched the situation with growing concern. Many Americans felt a strong sympathy for France and England because of historic or cultural ties. Yet some Americans of German, Irish, and other ancestry supported Germany. Woodrow Wilson urged the country to remain neutral. Indeed, many citizens favored isolationism for the United States, believing that we should keep to ourselves and let Europe work out its own problems. That idea soon was shattered by a terrifying new weapon unleashed by the Germans—the U-boat.

Germany did not invent the submarine, but it was the first nation to use it on a large scale in wartime. In answer to Britain's naval blockade of Germany, these U-boats (undersea boats) began attacking without warning any ship approaching or leaving Great Britain. On May 7, 1915, the unarmed British passenger ship Lusitania was torpedoed by a U-boat and sunk off the Irish coast. Among the 1,198 people who died were 128 Americans.

The United States was outraged. Many citizens demanded prompt revenge, but President Wilson refused to commit his nation to the years of bloodshed that would follow a declaration of war. He assured his angry compatriots that there was such a thing as being "too proud to fight." Not everyone agreed, but Germany did eventually restrict its U-boat attacks. Meanwhile, Wilson worked to bring the warring nations together to talk out their differences. Despite his efforts, the conflict raged on.

Most Americans were satisfied with their president's peacetime leadership. In 1916, they reelected Wilson because, as his campaign slogan proclaimed, "he kept us out of war." Still fearing that the United States would be drawn into the fighting before it ended, Wilson proposed a "peace without victory" early the following year. By this he hoped to avoid the bitter feelings caused by "a victor's terms imposed upon the vanquished."

Yet the Great War moved relentlessly closer. Within days of Wilson's plea for peace without victory, Germany again stepped up its submarine offensive. Soon afterward, a secret telegram came to light that outlined a German plot to draw Mexico into the war against the United States. And when the Kaiser's U-boats sank three U.S. merchant ships in March, President Wilson could hold out no longer. On April 2, 1917, he appeared before Congress.

Name _____

Date _____ Class _____

Denouncing the German U-boat campaign, Wilson declared his willingness to fight. "We will not choose the path of submission and suffer the most sacred rights of our nation and our people to be ignored or violated," he said. "The world must be made safe for democracy."

Now the United States scrambled to build a war machine from the ground up. Wilson selected able men such as General John J. Pershing to lead the fighting overseas and future president Herbert Hoover to direct civilian agencies at home. In a year, the United States was at full combat strength.

World War I was forcing changes in the United States. As president, Woodrow Wilson faced choices never before encountered by a chief executive. As a nation, the United States paid a bitter price to learn that its position as a world power brought responsibilities that could not be ignored.

Handout 1C: Fluency Homework

Directions:

1. Day 1: Read the text carefully and annotate to help you read fluently.

2. Each day:
   a. Practice reading the text aloud three to five times.
   b. Evaluate your progress by placing a checkmark in the appropriate, unshaded box.
   c. Ask someone (adult or peer) to listen and evaluate you as well.

3. Last day: Answer the self-reflection question at the end.

Since the United States traded with both the Allies and the Central Powers, President Woodrow Wilson tried to maintain U.S. neutrality. But to combat a British naval blockade of continental Europe, Germany used a new weapon, the *Unterseeboot*, or U-boat. While underwater, this submarine was able to launch torpedoes that could sink enemy ships. In May 1915, the British cruise ship Lusitania, which was carrying American passengers, was sunk. When outraged Americans called for war, President Wilson's strong protests to Germany resulted in a temporary halt to U-boat attacks on passenger vessels and neutral merchant ships, and the United States stayed out of the war.

U.S. neutrality did not last, however. Sabotage orchestrated by the German ambassador in America and the resumption of U-boat activity forced President Wilson to act. On April 6, 1917, the United States entered the conflict, with Wilson declaring that "the world must be made safe for democracy."

Zuber, Shari Lyn. "The War to End All Wars"

Student Performance Checklist:	Day 1		Day 2		Day 3		Day 4	
	You	Listener*	You	Listener*	You	Listener*	You	Listener*
Accurately read the passage three to five times.								
Read with appropriate phrasing and pausing.								
Read with appropriate expression.								
Read articulately at a good pace and an audible volume.								

*Adult or peer

Self-reflection: What choices did you make about tone and appropriate expression when deciding how to read this passage, and why? What would you like to improve on or try differently next time?

Handout 2A: Choosing Evidence for Concision and Precision

Directions: Fill in the definitions of concision and precision, read the examples, and respond to the questions and prompt.

Concision means _____.

Precision means _____.

Shari Lyn Zuber writes about the United States and World War I: "<u>Since the United States traded with both the Allies and the Central Powers</u>, President Woodrow Wilson tried to maintain U.S. neutrality. But to combat a British naval blockade of continental Europe, Germany used a new weapon, the Unterseeboot, or U-boat. While underwater, this submarine was able to launch torpedoes that could sink enemy ships. In May 1915, the British cruise ship Lusitania, which was carrying American passengers, was sunk. When outraged Americans called for war, President Wilson's strong protests to Germany resulted in a temporary halt to U-boat attacks on passenger vessels and neutral merchant ships, and the United States stayed out of the war." Zuber continues: "U.S. neutrality did not last, however. Sabotage orchestrated by the German ambassador in America and the resumption of U-boat activity forced President Wilson to act. On April 6, 1917, the United States entered the conflict, with Wilson declaring that 'the world must be made safe for democracy.'"	The United States joined World War I later than many other countries. <u>The United States President promoted neutrality</u>. There was a deciding factor that changed things for the United States. This incident transformed the "Peace President" (Zuber). The United States entered the war.

Name _____

Date _____ Class _____

What do you notice about the example above in relation to concision? What is the effect on the reader?	What do you notice about the example above in relation to precision? What is the effect on the reader?

Using information from the two examples above, create one new example that quotes evidence with concision to add precision to your ideas.

Name _____

Date _____ Class _____

Handout 5A: Collect Evidence: Two Perspectives

Directions: Complete the task below in preparation for writing your Focusing Question Task, in which you will explain two perspectives for joining World War I. Write responses using phrases rather than full sentences.

Complete the following charts using information from two or more of the following texts:

"The War to End All Wars," Shari Lyn Zuber (Handout 1A)

"The Peace President Goes to War," Duane Damon (Handout 1B)

"The Teenage Soldiers of World War One," BBC

"Your Country Needs You: Why Did So Many Volunteer in 1914?," Toby Thacker

Perspective: British Men

What do I need to know?	What kind of evidence could help me answer the question?	What information did I find?
Who was involved?		
When did they join?		
Why did they join—what was their motivation?		

Name _____

Date _____ Class _____

Now, place an asterisk next to the most important evidence for developing your explanation of why British men joined the war. Be sure your choices include at least two different types of evidence: fact, statistic, definition, general explanation/description, first-person account, claim.

Perspective: The United States

What do I need to know?	What kind of evidence could help me answer the question?	What information did I find?
Who was involved?		
When did they join?		
Why did they join–what was their motivation?		

Now, place an asterisk next to the most important evidence for developing your explanation of why America joined the war. Be sure your choices include at least two different types of evidence: fact, statistic, definition, general explanation/description, first-person account, claim.

Handout 6A: Military Vocabulary

Part I – Directions: Choose three of the words in the word bank to use to answer the questions below. Verify definitions with a dictionary.

ration (n.) – page 1	billets (n.) – page 7	sector (n.) – page 2
quartermaster (n.) – page 2	queue (n.) – page 4	issues (n.) – page 5
latrine (n.) – page 7	barracks (n.) – page 7	recruits (n.) – page 7

1. The first word I am going to examine is _____ .

Are there context clues for this word, and if so, what are they?

_____

What do I predict the meaning of the word is?

_____

Does that definition fit into the context of the sentences?

_____

How important is the word to my overall understanding of the plot?

_____

2. The second word I am going to examine is _____ .

Are there context clues for this word, and if so, what are they?

_____

Name _____

Date _____ Class _____

What do I predict the meaning of the word is?

_____

Does that definition fit into the context of the sentences?

_____

How important is the word to my overall understanding of the plot?

_____

3. The third word I am going to examine is _____ .

Are there context clues for this word, and if so, what are they?

_____

What do I predict the meaning of the word is?

_____

Does that definition fit into the context of the sentences?

_____

How important is the word to my overall understanding of the plot?

_____

Part II – Directions: Using at least two of the terms from the word bank and two of the rankings from the start of the lesson, write a short paragraph correctly using each word.

_____

Handout 7A: Fluency Homework

Directions:

1. Day 1: Read the text carefully and annotate to help you read fluently.
2. Each day:
   a. Practice reading the text aloud three to five times.
   b. Evaluate your progress by placing a check mark in the appropriate, unshaded box.
   c. Ask someone (adult or peer) to listen and evaluate you as well.
3. Last day: Answer the self-reflection question at the end.

For us lads of eighteen they ought to have been mediators and guides to the world of maturity, the world of work, of duty, of culture, of progress–to the future. We often made fun of them and played jokes on them, but in our hearts we trusted them. The idea of authority, which they represented, was associated in our minds with a greater insight and a more humane wisdom. But the first death we saw shattered this belief. We had to recognize that our generation was more to be trusted than theirs. They surpassed us only in phrases and in cleverness. The first bombardment showed us our mistake, and under it the world as they had taught it to us broke in pieces.

Remarque, Erich Maria. *All Quiet on the Western Front.*

New York: Ballantine, 1929. 12–13.

Student Performance Checklist:	Day 1		Day 2		Day 3		Day 4	
	You	Listener*	You	Listener*	You	Listener*	You	Listener*
Accurately read the passage three to five times.								
Read with appropriate phrasing and pausing.								
Read with appropriate expression.								
Read articulately at a good pace and an audible volume.								

*Adult or peer

Self-reflection: What choices did you make about tone and appropriate expression when deciding how to read this passage, and why? What would you like to improve on or try differently next time?

Handout 8A: Broad Category Organization

Directions: Read the examples below and answer the following questions.

Example 1	Example 2
Paul experiences comradeship and loss of innocence in the incidents of chapters 1 and 2 of *All Quiet on the Western Front*. For example, after enlisting in the army Paul made many new friends, including Kat and Detering. Paul says that "comradeship" is "the finest thing that arose out of the war" (27). However, Paul also sees many horrible things that cause him to lose the innocence of his youth and feel like "old folk" (18). In *All Quiet on the Western Front*, both comradeship and loss of innocence affect Paul. Kemmerich experiences comradeship and loss of innocence in the incidents of chapters 1 and 2 of *All Quiet on the Western Front*. When he is in the dressing station, he relies on his friends to help him. Kemmerich's loss of innocence is clear right before his death. He knows he is going to die and "cries" silently (31). He is no longer the little boy Paul knew in school. In *All Quiet on the Western Front*, both comradeship and loss of innocence affect Kemmerich.	The incidents in chapters 1 and 2 of *All Quiet on the Western Front* show how comradeship is important to men in the Second Company. The men face many challenges in the military, and in order to stay safe and healthy they need to rely on one another. For instance, Kemmerich relies on his friends to bring him his things when he is in the dressing station. Also, the friendship of the soldiers is important to Paul when his friend Kropp stands up to the mean Corporal Himmelstoss and ends the corporal's "authority" over the men (25). As a result of comradeship in the incidents in the novel so far, the soldiers are able to live a little better despite the difficult circumstances. The incidents in chapters 1 and 2 of *All Quiet on the Western Front* confirm the loss of innocence of the soldiers in the Second Company. Paul cannot "comprehend" his former life and says he is "cut off" from the student he used to be at home (19). In addition, Kemmerich loses his foot. Before he dies, he weeps because he is "entirely alone" (31). Both of these examples show how the Iron Youth, the students who became soldiers, lose their innocence because of the war.

What do you notice about how these examples are organized?

_____

_____

Which example is a more effective explanation of comradeship and loss of innocence? Why?

_____

_____

Handout 9A: Broad Category Evidence Organization

Directions: Cut each piece of text evidence into a separate strip. Evaluate each piece of evidence, and group related evidence by stacking strips into different piles.

"Our early life is cut off from the moment we came here, and that without our lifting a hand" (19).

"We stick out our chests, shave in the open, shove our hands in our pockets, inspect the recruits and feel ourselves stone-age veterans" (35).

"In time things far worse than that came easy to us" (8).

"The rain becomes heavier, we take out our waterproof sheets and spread them over our heads" (73).

"The war swept us away. For the others, the older men, it is but an interruption" (24).

"We are no longer soldiers but little more than boys; no one would believe that we could carry packs" (29).

"We were all at once terribly alone; and alone we must see it through" (13).

"the white butterflies flutter around and float on the soft warm wind of the late summer" (9).

"There is a smell of tar, of summer, and of sweaty feet" (40)

Name _____

Date _____ Class _____

Handout 11A: Text Analysis

Directions: Reread and discuss the following questions in your Expert Group before returning to your squad. Record your answers in your Response Journal.

Expert Group 1

In your small group, reread pages 67–70 aloud, from "But the shelling is stronger than everything" to "the wave sweeps over me and extinguishes me," rotating readers after each paragraph. After rereading, answer the following questions.

1. How does Paul describe the gas? Does his description affect your understanding of the conditions on the front?

2. How do the bombardment and gas attack develop the idea of camaraderie on the front?

Expert Group 2

In your small group, reread pages 70–73 aloud, from "The shelling has ceased" to "Young innocents" rotating readers each paragraph. After rereading, answer the following questions.

1. What decision does Kat make in response to the encounter with the wounded recruit? Why does he make this decision?

2. How do Paul's and Kat's reactions to the wounded recruit reveal how conditions on the front impact the men of the Second Company?

Expert Group 3

In your small group, reread pages 73–74 aloud, from "Our losses are less" to "'we are again half asleep,'" rotating readers each paragraph. After rereading, answer the following questions.

1. On whom does the rain fall? How does the rain develop the experience of being at war?

2. What is the effect of the repetition of the word *monotonously* (74)?

Handout 12A: "Fighting From the Trenches," Kathryn M. Horst

Directions: Follow along as you listen to a Read Aloud.

Imagine a six-foot ditch weaving from Washington, D.C., to Detroit, Michigan. Men's heads could not be seen over the top edges. Dugouts would be tunneled for sleeping and eating quarters.

Such a system of trenches was used on a grand scale during World War I. The armies of the Central Powers (Germany and Austria-Hungary) and the Allies (Great Britain, France, Russia, and later the United States) dug rifle pits and foxholes from which to shoot. Soon the men connected these ditches, forming a long, deep fighting line. These trenches crossed rivers, farmland, forests, and mountains.

Two front lines were established. The western front stretched five hundred miles from Belgium to Switzerland. The eastern front, between Germany and Russia, extended about eleven hundred miles from the Baltic Sea to the Black Sea. In the beginning of the war, the Germans and Allies hurried to outdig each other to establish these strongholds.

Many important battles were fought during World War I, but there was constant fighting between Allied and German soldiers in the trenches. In some places, opposing trenches were only a few yards apart, and enemy soldiers could talk to each other. In other places, trenches were separated by as much as a mile.

As World War I continued, the German and Allied trenches became more elaborate. Earth was mounded in front as a ridge, or parapet. Men stood on shelves, or steps, dug in the sides for shooting. Some trenches were wide enough for two men to pass or to allow donkeys to walk through carrying packs. Concrete slabs reinforced the walls. Wooden walkways lined the bottom. Men shoveled out cavelike rooms called pillboxes. The Germans dug trenches as deep as forty feet and even wired some with electricity for washing and cooking. Once the Allies even dug a long, deep tunnel to the German front to lay land mines.

Often behind the front lines, soldiers built second and third support trenches for added protection. Underground tunnels connected these lines. There soldiers carried shells, wire, food, and coal. First-aid stations, soldiers' quarters, kitchens, and ammunition stores all were underground.

Troops and supplies moved to the front by a zigzag line called a communication trench. Soldiers carrying food to the front lines had to be extremely careful, as they were sure targets for enemy attack. As a result, the art of camouflage, or disguise, was developed. During the war, camouflaged clothing, hide-outs, and trap doors saved lives.

Trench warfare was constant, with day and night artillery firings shaking the ground. Machine guns that automatically fired three hundred shots per minute hurt the men's ears. Grenades and shell attacks transformed night into day. A continual fear of noise, or shell shock, affected many soldiers. With such enormous bombardments, it was difficult for either side to make headway. The men were bored; no one could advance.

At times soldiers were moved to a quiet sector, a trench line where the Germans and Allies agreed to rest. Toul, France, was such a location. There the men relaxed, finally getting away from the steady gunfire. It seemed like heaven.

The most difficult order for soldiers was "over the top." When they heard that cry, they crawled out of the ditches and attacked the enemy. It was almost certain death because of enemy firing and because the area between the Allied and German lines was covered with hundreds of feet of barbed wire, mounded dirt, and land mines.

This "no man's land" was constructed to slow down attacks. Often the barbed wire collapsed during one attack and was rebuilt overnight. No man's land usually was stripped of trees and vegetation. Crater fields from the bombings pocketed the ground.

Thousands of men lived in trenches like gophers, enduring many hardships. Soldiers had short haircuts so no cooties, or lice, would burrow there. Rats and roaches infested the sleeping quarters. Snails dug holes in the dirt walls. Because of the damp European climate, water and mud could be knee deep. In times of attack, wounded men could not crawl up the slippery sides and had to lie in the muck. Soldiers later improvised pumps to help drain the ditches, and the army soon issued thigh-high boots.

Rainy weather exposed men to diseases such as influenza, pneumonia, and skin afflictions. New ailments such as trench foot, trench mouth, and trench fever evolved.

During the four years of World War I, more than ten million soldiers fought and died. Many more million were hurt or disabled. Ironically, neither the Allied nor German trench lines advanced more than ten miles, and in many cases, the trenches never were redug toward the enemy line. Because of this type of warfare, billions of dollars were spent on ammunition. Natural resources, such as steel and copper, were depleted in all the warring countries.

World War I ended on November 11, 1918. Over the years, many trenches have been plowed under, built upon, or covered by wild grasses and flowers. But some still remain as a grim reminder of the devastation of the war.

Name _____

Date _____ Class _____

Handout 12B: Fluency Homework

Directions:

1. Read the text carefully and annotate to help you read fluently.

2. Each day:
   a. Practice reading the text aloud three to five times.
   b. Evaluate your progress by placing a checkmark in the appropriate, unshaded box.
   c. Ask someone (adult or peer) to listen and evaluate you as well.

3. Last day: Answer the self-reflection question at the end.

From the earth, from the air, sustaining forces pour into us—mostly from the earth. To no man does the earth mean so much as to the soldier. When he presses himself down upon her long and powerfully, when he buries his face and his limbs deep in her from the fear of death by shell-fire, then she is his only friend, his brother, his mother; he stifles his terror and his cries in her silence and her security; she shelters him and releases him for ten seconds to live, to run, ten seconds of life; receives him again and often for ever.

Remarque, Erich Maria. *All Quiet on the Western Front.*

New York: Ballantine, 1929. 55.

Student Performance Checklist:	Day 1		Day 2		Day 3		Day 4	
	You	Listener*	You	Listener*	You	Listener*	You	Listener*
Accurately read the passage three to five times.								
Read with appropriate phrasing and pausing.								
Read with appropriate expression.								
Read articulately at a good pace and an audible volume.								

*Adult or peer

Self-reflection: What choices did you make about tone and appropriate expression when deciding how to read this passage, and why? What would you like to improve on or try differently next time?

Handout 12C: Multiple Meaning Chart

Part 1 – Directions: Write *elaborate* in the oval, and write a different definition in each box to show the multiple meanings of the word. Then, write a sentence for each definition of the word on the lines beneath each box.

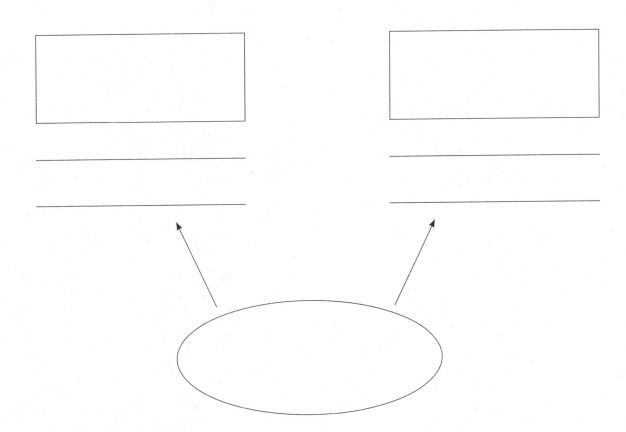

Part 2 – Directions: Answer the question below in complete sentences.

Which definition best fits your inference about the meaning of elaborate in "Fighting From the Trenches"? Explain your answer.

Handout 13A: Transitions in Writing

Directions: Use this guide to help you identify and incorporate transitional expressions in your writing.

Function	Examples
Agreement and Addition of Ideas	similarly, furthermore, in the same way, likewise, also, in addition, too, correspondingly, as well as, especially
Difference of Ideas	however, although, yet, on the contrary, others say, some might argue, nonetheless, but, on the other hand, instead, rather
Sequence or List	First, second, third, then, next, afterwards, after, last, until, before, after, meanwhile, in the past, recently, now
Show Significance	in fact, truly, indeed, without exception, most importantly, to emphasize
Cause and Effect	as a result, therefore, accordingly, thus, in this case, for this reason, because, consequently
Provide an Example	for example, for instance, to illustrate, including, in particular, for instance, to put another way, that is to say, with this in mind, in fact, to demonstrate, specifically
Conclusion or Summary	in conclusion, to summarize, in the end, when it is all said and done, finally, all together, overall

Handout 14A: Transitions Experiment

Directions: Read the paragraph below and, using the Transitions Key beneath the paragraph, add the appropriate transitions to create cohesion. Then share your paragraph with a partner and compare your use of transitions. Remember to refer to Handout 13A for different types of transitions.

Helplessness is a central idea that explains the experiences of the soldiers in *All Quiet on the Western Front*. _____ (1), the soldiers do not have control over their actions on the front or in training camp. They are told where to go and what to do by their commanding officers. _____ (2), they are even made to do pointless drills and exercises that do not prepare them for the harsh life on the front. _____ (3), the soldiers resent their superior officers and believe the "wrong people do the fighting" (41). _____ (4), this helplessness prevents the soldiers from doing what they think is right. When the fair-headed recruit is injured after the bombardment, Kat and Paul know that he will face "intolerable pain" (72) and want to end his life quickly. _____ (5), they are not allowed to kill a fellow soldier and are helpless in this situation. _____ (6), the soldiers are helpless in many different situations in *All Quiet on the Western Front*, and this increases the difficulty of life on the front.

Transitions Key

1. Provide an Example transition
2. Agreement and Addition of Ideas transition
3. Cause and Effect transition
4. Show Significance transition
5. Difference of Ideas transition
6. Conclusion or Summary transition

Name _____

Date _____ Class _____

Handout 14B: Descriptive and Sensory Details

Directions: Review pages 99–123 from *All Quiet on the Western Front* and "Fighting From the Trenches." Record the five most significant descriptive and sensory details about conditions on the front from each text in the appropriate column. Then respond to the short-answer questions below.

Chapter 6, *All Quiet on the Western Front*	"Fighting From the Trenches"
1.	1.
2.	2.
3.	3.
4.	4.
5.	5.
How do details from this portion of chapter 6 illuminate conditions on the front?	How do details in "Fighting From the Trenches" illuminate conditions on the front?

Handout 16A: Collect Evidence–Conditions on the Front

Directions: Now that you have chosen to write about either Kropp or Müller, review the evidence from the status reports. Choose two incidents or conversations about your character's experiences on the front with specific lines of dialogue that involve your chosen character, and write them in the chart below. Then, respond to the questions below.

Finally, identify at least three significant details from either Not So Quiet and/or "Fighting from the Trenches" that connect to your incidents or conversations and convey what life was like for soldiers fighting at the front. Review your previous work with descriptive details and sensory language for ideas.

Character's Name:	
Incident or Conversation 1	
What does this incident reveal about this character? • How did the character respond? • What does the incident reveal about how conditions on the front affect that character?	
Incident or Conversation 2	

Name

Date　　　　　　　　　　　Class

What does this incident reveal about this character? • How did the character respond? • What does the incident reveal about how conditions on the front affect that character?	
Related Details from Supplementary Texts: • Remember to record the source text for these details!	

Handout 18A: Fluency Homework

Directions:
1. Day 1: Read the text carefully and annotate to help you read fluently.

2. Each day:
    a. Practice reading the text aloud three to five times.
    b. Evaluate your progress by placing a checkmark in the appropriate, unshaded box.
    c. Ask someone (adult or peer) to listen and evaluate you as well.

3. Last day: Answer the self-reflection question at the end.

Dulce et Decorum Est

Bent double, like old beggars under sacks,
Knock-kneed, coughing like hags, we cursed through sludge,
Till on the haunting flares we turned our backs,
And towards our distant rest began to trudge.
Men marched asleep. Many had lost their boots,
But limped on, blood-shod. All went lame; all blind;
Drunk with fatigue; deaf even to the hoots
Of gas-shells dropping softly behind.

Gas! GAS! Quick, boys!—An ecstasy of fumbling
Fitting the clumsy helmets just in time,
But someone still was yelling out and stumbling
And flound'ring like a man in fire or lime.—
Dim through the misty panes and thick green light,
As under a green sea, I saw him drowning.

In all my dreams before my helpless sight,
He plunges at me, guttering, choking, drowning.

If in some smothering dreams, you too could pace
Behind the wagon that we flung him in,
And watch the white eyes writhing in his face,
His hanging face, like a devil's sick of sin;
If you could hear, at every jolt, the blood
Come gargling from the froth-corrupted lungs,
Obscene as cancer, bitter as the cud
Of vile, incurable sores on innocent tongues,—
My friend, you would not tell with such high zest
To children ardent for some desperate glory,
The old Lie: Dulce et decorum est
Pro patria mori.

Owen, Wilfred. *Poetry Foundation.*
n.d., Web.

Name _____

Date _____ Class _____

Student Performance Checklist:	Day 1		Day 2		Day 3		Day 4	
	You	Listener*	You	Listener*	You	Listener*	You	Listener*
Accurately read the passage three to five times.								
Read with appropriate phrasing and pausing.								
Read with appropriate expression.								
Read articulately at a good pace and an audible volume.								

*Adult or peer

Self-reflection: What choices did you make about tone and appropriate expression when deciding how to read this passage, and why? What would you like to improve on or try differently next time?

Handout 18B: Fluency Homework

Directions:

1. Day 1: Read the text carefully and annotate to help you read fluently.

2. Each day:
    a. Practice reading the text aloud three to five times.
    b. Evaluate your progress by placing a checkmark in the appropriate, unshaded box.
    c. Ask someone (adult or peer) to listen and evaluate you as well.

3. Last day: Answer the self-reflection question at the end.

In Flanders Fields

In Flanders fields the poppies blow
Between the crosses, row on row,
That mark our place; and in the sky
The larks, still bravely singing, fly
Scarce heard amid the guns below.

We are the Dead. Short days ago
We lived, felt dawn, saw sunset glow,
Loved and were loved, and now we lie,
In Flanders fields.

Take up our quarrel with the foe:
To you from failing hands we throw
The torch; be yours to hold it high.
If ye break faith with us who die
We shall not sleep, though poppies grow
In Flanders fields.

McCrae, John. *Poetry Foundation*.
n.d., Web.

Name _____

Date _____ Class _____

Student Performance Checklist:	Day 1		Day 2		Day 3		Day 4	
	You	Listener*	You	Listener*	You	Listener*	You	Listener*
Accurately read the passage three to five times.								
Read with appropriate phrasing and pausing.								
Read with appropriate expression.								
Read articulately at a good pace and an audible volume.								

*Adult or peer

Self-reflection: What choices did you make about tone and appropriate expression when deciding how to read this passage, and why? What would you like to improve on or try differently next time?

Name

Date   Class

Handout 21A: Film Techniques

Directions: Employ these terms in your analysis of the films. Annotate key points on the handout and add your own notes.

As you analyze shots and scenes, ask:
How does a film technique affect

- My reaction to a scene or shot?
- My understanding of the central focus or subject?
- My understanding of the meaning?

Name

Date   Class

Visual Technique	Characteristics and Effects
Shot Selection Each shot <u>frames</u> what the viewer sees. Shots structure the content of the film and create a relationship between the viewer and the film's subject. Directors use many different types of shots in filmmaking.	These three terms describe **the distance** between the camera and its subject: **Close-up:** Emphasizes details, with the subject filling most of the frame. Think of a shot of a person's head from the neck up or of a melting hot fudge sundae. A close-up indicates the importance of the subject. For example, a close-up on a person's expression draws attention to the importance of what the person is feeling, thinking, or saying. A close-up emphasizes emotion, often creating an emotional response in the viewer. Think of what it feels like to be very close to something: A close-up can be used to make the viewer feel very comfortable or uncomfortable about a character or subject. **Medium shot:** Frames about half of the subject. With people, the shot is often from the waist up. There is a medium distance between viewer and scene; think of it as halfway between a close up and a long shot. **Long shot or wide shot**: Extends the distance by showing the foreground and the background. It creates a broad picture that can emphasize the distance between things, or create a relationship between different things in the frame. A long shot is often used to indicate where the story is taking place or to frame a character in a setting. A long shot orients the viewer by conveying where the story is occurring. Unlike the close-up, which emphasizes emotion, the long shot shows action. Other shots: **Shot/counter shot or shot reverse shot**: A series that views the action from one side (the shot) and then the opposite side (the counter shot or reverse shot). Often used in a conversation between characters, with the first shot showing a character looking at another character (who is off-screen) and then the counter shot showing the other character looking back at the first character. This series can show the point of view of two different characters. **Reaction shot**: Show the effects of someone's actions or words on others.

Name _____

Date _____ Class _____

Camera Angle	**High angle:** The camera is positioned above the action or scene. The angle looks down on the subject, which tends to make the subject seem small, insignificant, weak, or inferior.
The angle refers to the specific <u>location</u> at which the camera is placed to take the shot. Directors use different angles to frame the scene, the action, and the characters.	<ul><li>Bird's-eye view–angle is from directly overhead, like a bird flying over the scene. Often used to make humans seem insignificant in relationship to the setting–the size of ants.</li><li>Aerial shot–describes an angle from the air–often from higher up than a bird, as from an airplane or satellite in space. An aerial shot can establish the setting by providing an overview of the scene.</li></ul>**Eye-level:** A common view that represents a real-world angle of how a viewer would see the scene in real life. Considered a "neutral" shot because it doesn't frame the subject in an unusual way. Eye-level angles can be used to make the viewer feel like he or she is part of the scene. **Low angle:** The camera looks up at the subject from below. This angle can make the subject appear powerful, ominous, or aggressive. It can inspire fear, awe, or disorientation in the viewer as he or she is dominated by what's on screen. **Oblique angle:** The camera is deliberately tilted, or slanted, to one side for dramatic effect. Can portray disorientation, instability, frantic action, etc. Sometimes used to convey a character's point of view on a scene. **Wide angle:** Another term for long or wide shot.

Name _____

Date _____ Class _____

Editing and Camera Movement	Editing together a series of short shots is like taking a series of photographs. A series of quick cuts can make the action seem fast-paced and intense, as in a series that cuts from a menacing figure in the distance to the next shot of the character in the foreground of the scene.
A film is made by joining shots together in an editing process.	
A film director and editor make a series of cuts that join one shot to the next.	In the same film, the director can take a much longer shot, with the camera recording uninterrupted action, like taking a video. This technique can make it seem as if the action takes longer, as it takes time to unfold.
	Types of longer single shots:
	- **Pan:** A stationary camera turns horizontally (left or right) following an object or scene.
	- **Tilt:** A stationary camera turns up or down following an object or scene.
	- **Zoom:** A stationary camera uses a special lens to zoom in or out on a subject.
	- **Tracking shot:** The camera moves with the action, often following a character. The camera can move left or right or forward and backward. It creates a sense of movement that can emphasize the action, creating different effects in the viewer: exhilaration, dizziness, or anticipation.
Lighting	The use of natural or artificial lighting to create emphasis on particular figures or objects in a shot.
	- Shadow can be used to convey evil, mystery, or a dark mood.
	- Bright lighting of a character may suggest their goodness, happiness, or importance.
	- Contrasts in lighting can highlight differences between characters, objects, or places in a shot or scene

Name _____

Date _____ Class _____

Sound Technique	Characteristics and Effects
Diegetic Sound	Sounds that occur <u>within</u> the action of the story. They include: Characters' voices and dialogue. Sounds made by figures or objects (such as a door slamming). Background noises (such as wind howling).
Non-diegetic Sound	Sounds that occur <u>outside</u> of the story, or <u>off screen</u>. They include: Narration or voiceover. Musical soundtrack.
All sound	**Timing:** When a sound appears, how long it lasts, and how much it matches or differs from what the viewer sees, alerts the viewer to important moments and elements of the story. **Volume:** How loud or soft a sound is alerts the viewer to important moments and elements of the story. **Tone:** Helps establish a particular mood.

Acting	Characteristics and Effects
The way an actor behaves.	Acting includes: Physical movements. Facial expressions. Actions. Interactions with characters, objects, and surroundings. Many <u>external</u> actions can suggest the <u>internal</u> state of the character. For example, a character walking with long, determined strides can suggest confidence.

Handout 21B: Verb Voice T-Chart

Part 1

Directions: Sort the sentences on the board into the correct column.

Active	Passive

Part 2

Directions: Write an A in front of the sentence if the verb voice is active or a P if the verb voice is passive.

_____ 1. Himmelstoss was attacked by Paul and his friends.

_____ 2. The horrors of World War I inspired artists to show the brevity of life.

_____ 3. Paul is eventually found by his comrades after his encounter with the French soldier.

_____ 4. Survivors of the war were called the Lost Generation.

_____ 5. Artists created abstract and unconventional pieces.

Name _____

Date _____ Class _____

Handout 23A: Socratic Seminar Prewriting

Directions: Choose two or more of the following questions to respond to in your Response Journal. Use your notes, Response Journals, and any other information to formulate your responses. Your goal is to generate as many ideas as possible, so you may use phrases or bullet points, as well as full sentences, to construct your responses. Be sure you address at least two definitions of humanity in your prewriting.

1. What does the use of geometric shapes in Cubist painting reveal about the war's effect on humankind?

2. What do Paul's emotional responses to other characters (his friends, his family, the French soldier) convey about the war's effect on what it means to be human?

3. How does the film adaptation of *All Quiet on the Western Front* depict the enemy, and what does that depiction reveal about the role of humankind in warfare?

4. How do "In Flanders Fields" and "Dulce et Decorum Est" disagree in their views on the relationship between war and humanity?

5. What do one or more texts have to say about war's effects on humane compassion, or empathy, toward others? Toward oneself?

6. How do one or more texts depict the horrors of war and their effects on humankind? Human nature? Human compassion?

7. According to various texts, what does war reveal about human nature? Are humans essentially good or evil? Both? Neither?

8. According to various texts, what does war reveal about what makes us human?

9. How might war affect humanity in a positive way?

10. How does a text's genre (fiction, film, painting, poetry) contribute to your understanding of an idea about war and humanity?

Handout 23B: Verb Voice T-Chart

Part 1

Directions: Sort the sentences on the board into the correct column.

Active	Passive

Part 2

Directions: Write an A in front of the sentence is the verb voice is active or a P if the verb voice is passive.

_____ 1. Himmelstoss was attacked by Paul and his friends.

_____ 2. The horrors of World War I inspired artists to show the brevity of life.

_____ 3. Paul is eventually found by his comrades after his encounter with the French soldier.

_____ 4. Survivors of the war were called the Lost Generation.

_____ 5. Artists created abstract and unconventional pieces.

Handout 25A: Film Analysis: "Forgive Me, Comrade"

Directions: Work with your group members to formulate responses and collect evidence in preparation for writing your Focusing Question Task. In that task, you will evaluate the film's depiction of a scene from chapter 9, explaining how it depicts war's effect on humanity in comparison to the novel.

Follow these steps:

1. Take out Handout 21A: Film Techniques, and use the information to formulate your responses.
2. Watch the film excerpt "Forgive Me, Comrade."
3. Summarize what is happening in the scene:

4. Assign each group member a category: visual techniques, sound techniques, acting.
5. Watch the film clip again, taking notes on the significant choices made in your category in the chart below.

   As you watch, pay attention to the choices that depict
   - Aspects of Paul's character.
   - The relationship between Paul and the soldier.
   - The setting.

   Consider:
   - Does the scene focus on action? Emotion? Both? When does it change?

6. Repeat step 5, rotating categories, so each group member takes notes on a different category. For example, if you took notes on sound during the last screening, take notes on visual techniques during this one.

"Forgive Me, Comrade" from *All Quiet on the Western Front*, dir. Lewis Milestone (1930)

Name _____

Date _____ Class _____

1. Visual techniques

Shot selection	
Camera angles	
Camera movement	
Editing	
Lighting	

Name _____

Date _____ Class _____

2. Sound techniques

Sound Effects	
Voice: dialogue or narration	

3. Acting

Physical movements	
Facial expressions	
Actions	
Interactions with characters, objects, and surroundings	

7. Now, brainstorm with your group members to respond to the following questions:

What are the most significant choices the filmmaker and actors made in the depiction of the scene of Paul with the French soldier? Why?

What do these choices reveal about the film's attitudes toward war and its effects on humanity? Be sure to review the definitions of humanity and specify which meaning you are using.

Handout 27A: Fluency Homework

Directions:

1. Day 1: Read the text carefully and annotate to help you read fluently.
2. Each day:
   a. Practice reading the text aloud three to five times.
   b. Evaluate your progress by placing a checkmark in the appropriate, unshaded box.
   c. Ask someone (adult or peer) to listen and evaluate you as well.
3. Last day: Answer the self-reflection question at the end.

The silence spreads. I talk and must talk. So I speak to him and to say to him: "Comrade, I did not want to kill you. If you jumped in here again, I would not do it, if you would be sensible, too. But you were only an idea to me before, an abstraction that lived in my mind and called forth its appropriate response. It was that abstraction I stabbed. But no, for the first time, I see you are a man like me. I thought of your hand-grenades, of your bayonet, of your rifle; now I see your wife and your face and our fellowship. Forgive me, comrade. We always see it too late. Why do they never tell us that you are poor devils like us, that your mothers are just as anxious as ours, and that we have the same fear of death, and the same dying and the same agony—Forgive me, comrade; how could you be my enemy? If we threw away these rifles and this uniform you could be my brother just like Kat and Albert. Take twenty years of my life, comrade, and stand up—take more, for I do not know what I can even attempt to do with it now.

Remarque, Erich Maria. *All Quiet on the Western Front*.
New York: Ballantine, 1929. 223.

Student Performance Checklist:	Day 1		Day 2		Day 3		Day 4	
	You	Listener*	You	Listener*	You	Listener*	You	Listener*
Accurately read the passage three to five times.								
Read with appropriate phrasing and pausing.								
Read with appropriate expression.								
Read articulately at a good pace and an audible volume.								

*Adult or peer

Self-reflection: What choices did you make about tone and appropriate expression when deciding how to read this passage, and why? What would you like to improve on or try differently next time?

Handout 29A: Text Analysis

Directions: Reread the appropriate section and discuss the following questions in your Expert Group before returning to your squad. Record your answers in your Response Journal.

Expert Group 1
In your small group, reread from "This is the mad story of Detering" to "We have heard nothing more of Detering" (275–77) aloud and answer the following questions. Recall the incident in paragraph 25 of "The teenage soldiers of World War One" to help you understand why Detering was court-martialed.

1. Why does Paul refer to this story about Detering as "mad" (275)?
2. Why does Detering pick the cherry blossoms?
3. How does Detering's decision in response to the cherry tree reveal a psychological effect?

Expert Group 2
In your small group, reread pages 277–279 from "But sometimes it broke out in other ways" to "gets a bullet in the leg while doing it" aloud and answer the following questions.

1. What is the "danger" Paul refers to in the story of Berger (277)?
2. Why do the men refer to Berger as "mad" (279)?
3. How does Berger's decision in response to the wounded messenger-dog reveal a psychological effect?

Expert Group 3
In your small group, reread pages 279–281 from "Müller is dead" to "'Germany ought to be empty soon,' says Kat" aloud and answer the following questions.

1. What do the soldiers have too much of? What do they have too little of?
2. What does Paul think the "people at home should be shown" (280)?
3. How does Paul's promise to Kat reveal psychological effects of war (279)?

Name

Date   Class

Expert Group 4

In your small group, reread pages 281–283 from "We have given up hope" to "there are no other possibilities" aloud and answer the following questions. The military has a code that describes whether or not a man is well enough to fight, "A1" means that he is.

1. Why does Paul refer to stories like Kat's as "honest" (282)?

2. How does Paul's description of the tanks reveal a psychological effect?

3. According to Paul, what "possibilities" are available to a soldier, and how do they develop the idea of the "hopeless struggle" (283, 282)?

Handout 31A: Frayer Models

Directions: Complete one Frayer Model for shell shock and one for hysteria, drawing on evidence from "The Forgotten Female Shell-Shock Victims of World War I."

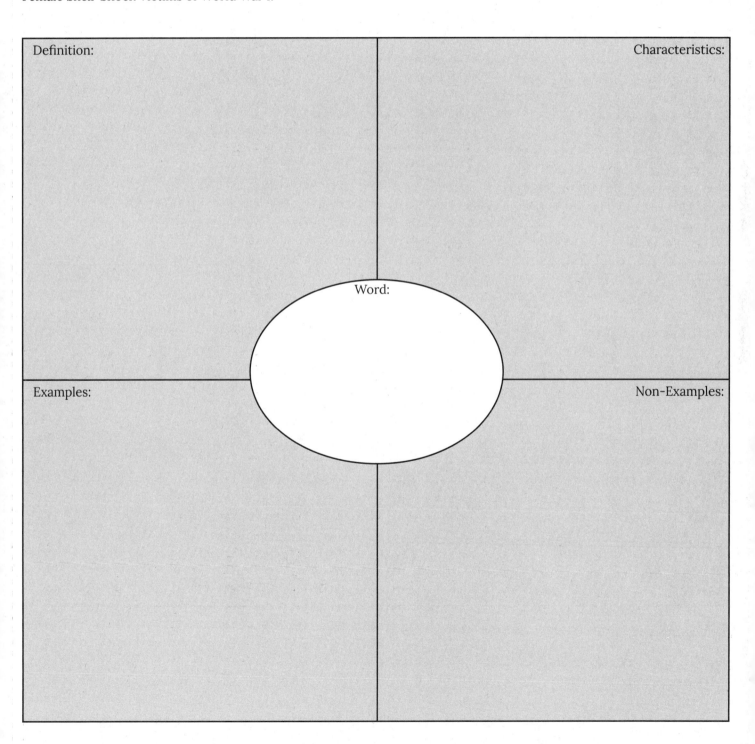

Name: _____

Date: _____ Class: _____

Definition:	Characteristics:
Examples:	Non-Examples:

Word:

Handout 32A: Using an Ellipsis

Part 1

Directions: Read the claim that the student wants to support in her essay. Then, review each piece of textual evidence she plans to use. Draw a line through text that does not support her claim and draw an ellipsis above the omitted text.

Claim: Paul and his fellow soldiers demonstrate how young men lost their humanity during the war.
Evidence 1: "We are insensible, dead men, who through some trick, some dreadful magic, are still able to run and kill" (116).
Evidence 2: "The blast of the hand-grenades impinges powerfully on our arms and legs; crouching like cats we run on, overwhelmed by this wave that bears us along, that fills us with ferocity, turns us into thugs, into murderers, into God only knows what devils" (114).

Part 2

Directions: Read the claim that the student wants to support in his essay. Then read the sentences from *All Quiet on the Western Front* that the student is considering using in his essay. Select the best quotation and write it on the lines below. Use an ellipsis to indicate portions of the quotation that do not support the student's claim.

Claim: Paul's growing disillusionment is presented through figurative language.
Evidence 1: "Leer groans as he supports himself on his arm, he bleeds quickly, no one can help him. Like an emptying tube, after a couple of minutes he collapses" (284).
Evidence 2: "Just as we turn into animals when we go up to the line, because that is the only thing which brings us through safely, so we turn into wags and loafers when we are resting" (138–139).
Evidence 3: "We will be superfluous even to ourselves, we will grow older, a few will adapt themselves, some others will merely submit, and most will be bewildered" (294).

Name _____

Date _____ Class _____

Handout 34A: End-of-Module Planning Packet

Directions: Step One: Review the Psychological Effects Anchor Chart and choose one effect to write about for your EOM Task. This effect will be your broad category. Complete a Frayer Model for your chosen effect below.

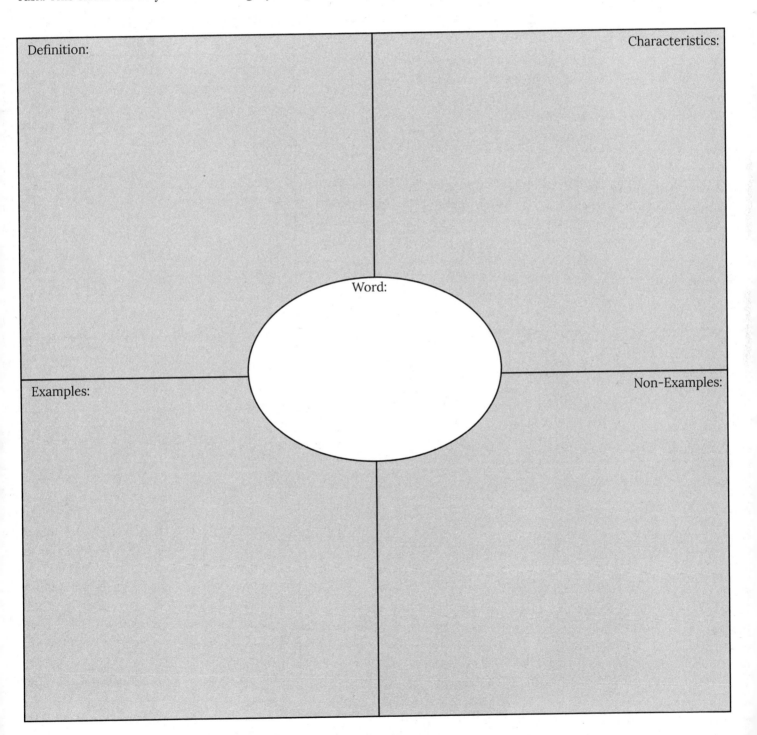

Name _____

Date _____ Class _____

Directions: Step Two: Identify five incidents from the novel that show your chosen effect. Choose examples from different points in the narrative, so that they represent beginning, middle, and end points of the narrative arc. Explain how these incidents affect Paul and how they develop your understanding of that effect overall.

Incident	How does this incident affect Paul? What is his response?	What does this incident reveal about your chosen effect?
1.		
2.		
3.		
4.		
5.		

Name _____

Date _____ Class _____

Directions: Step Three: Record the three incidents that offer the strongest evidence for your chosen effect, and provide a brief explanation of why each example is the strongest evidence.

Incident	This incident develops my chosen effect with the subcategory of …	This incident offers the strongest evidence because …
1.		
2.		
3.		

Directions: Step Four: Use the space below to draft your thesis statement.

Thesis Statement	

Directions: Step Five: Use the graphic organizer below to develop each of your two supporting paragraphs. Explain how each of your chosen incidents illustrates a subcategory of your effect and how that then develops your understanding of that effect.

Name _____

Date _____ Class _____

Thesis:		
Subcategory 1:		Subcategory 2:
Topic Statement:		Topic Statement:
Evidence:	Elaboration:	Evidence:	Elaboration:
Evidence:	Elaboration:	Evidence:	Elaboration:

Directions: Step Six: Conclude your essay by suggesting how your chosen effect illuminates a broader impact of World War I: its effect on society or the world, or on people's perception of an important idea, such as time, life, patriotism, or tradition.

Concluding Statement	

Handout 34B: End-of-Module Exemplar Essay

Directions: Read the following exemplar essay and use Handout 34C to identify successful and effective components of this response.

The Disease of War

Wilfred Owen's classic poem "Dulce et Decorum Est" illustrates the dark and terrible circumstances of World War I and the effects of that war on the speaker of the poem. The nightmarish episode described in the work is a gas attack, something common enough for a soldier on the front lines, but this attack takes the tired men by surprise and claims one victim. The speaker of the poem, weary and sick, cannot forget the dying man, who continues to haunt his dreams. This experience leaves him melancholy and embittered. World War I caused the lives of so many individuals to be destroyed as they were drafted or pressured to fight. The figurative language in "Dulce et Decorum Est" illustrates the speaker's feeling of powerlessness, a common psychological effect of individuals caught up in World War I who were ultimately crushed by modern warfare.

The speaker compares himself and his fellow soldiers to old men to show their helplessness. In the first stanza of "Dulce et Decorum Est," the speaker describes in detail his poor state and that of his fellow soldiers. A simile in the first line compares the physical condition of the soldiers to "old beggars" who are hunched and walking without strength (1). In the same way, the speaker of the poem further develops this physical weakness by saying the men "limped on" and were all "lame" (6). The speaker is one of these men, a man who, after his involvement in the fighting, is so beaten down and exhausted he cannot perform a basic function like walking properly. The speaker's inability to move is only one damaging effect of the war. The speaker's sense of hearing also has been damaged. The speaker is so tired that he is "deaf" to the sound of the "gas-shells" that threaten to kill (7, 8). By using the word "deaf," Owen shows that the effect on the speaker's senses is not temporary but a change that will last a lifetime (7). As a result of the atrocities of war, the soldiers' vitality is gone and they are now powerless old men.

This feeling of utter powerlessness is further developed in the poem through figurative language related to disease. The language of sickness illuminates the emotional ailments of war. In the fourth stanza, Owen uses similes and metaphors to describe the scarring image of the dying soldier. The sound of the dying man's lungs is like "gargling from froth-corrupted lungs…incurable sores on innocent tongues" (22–24). By saying the sores are "incurable," the speaker shows that, like cancer, they will never go away (24). Like the "corrupted" lungs, his memories will be forever distorted (22). These diseases mentioned in the poem change a body forever. Similarly, the war permanently changes the speaker, who sees the dying man in "all his dreams," indicating that he can never forget this horrifying experience (15). Most importantly, the speaker goes on to say the dreams are "smothering" because they are horrifying and oppressive (17). The speaker has been changed, yet he is aware there are still "children" who have not been broken by the war (26). The speaker wants others to avoid his experience, which proves to be toxic and unchangeable to not just his body, but his mind.

At the start of the poem "Dulce et Decorum Est," the speaker is already weak and lame because of his participation in World War I. After the gas attack and the dying man, the language of the poem makes comparisons to terminal, fatal diseases. By using such strong comparisons, the poem conveys the way the speaker has lost all his power and is

Name _____

Date _____ Class _____

completely destroyed—physically and emotionally—by his experiences. Thankfully, the speaker's reference to "children" indicates some kind of hope that other generations might be spared the feelings of total powerlessness (26). Ultimately, the speaker's wish is to dispel the idea that war is noble by allowing the reader a glimpse into the effects of the conflict on the men who had to fight in the trenches.

Handout 34C: Explanatory Writing Checklist

Directions: Use the following checklist as you deconstruct Handout 36B: End-of-Module Exemplar Essay and to assess your own explanatory essay.

Grade 8 Explanatory Writing Checklist	Self +/ Δ	Peer +/ Δ	Teacher +/ Δ
Reading Comprehension			
▪ I include three incidents that reveal a psychological effect of the war on Paul in *All Quiet on the Western Front*.			
▪ I identify connections between incidents that reveal a psychological effect in *All Quiet on the Western Front* to develop subcategories.			
▪ I demonstrate how three incidents of *All Quiet on the Western Front* develop a psychological effect of war on Paul.			
Structure			
▪ I respond to all parts of the prompt.			
▪ I focus on my psychological effect throughout the piece.			
▪ I introduce the psychological effect clearly in my introduction paragraph.			
▪ My introduction paragraph gives some kind of preview of the rest of the piece and includes a thesis that "sets the stage" or states the significance of my category.			
▪ I organize my ideas and subcategories clearly in body paragraphs.			
▪ My conclusion paragraph supports the focus and states the larger implications or "so what" of my category.			
▪ I use transitions to smoothly and logically connect paragraphs and ideas.			
Development			
▪ I develop my topic with sufficient evidence from *All Quiet on the Western Front*.			
▪ My evidence is relevant to the category.			
▪ I elaborate upon evidence by analyzing it accurately.			

Name _____

Date _____ Class _____

Style			
• I use a variety of sentence patterns (simple, compound, complex, compound-complex) to add clarity and interest to my writing.			
• I use vocabulary words that are specific and appropriate to the content.			
• I write precisely and concisely, without using unnecessary words.			
• I write in an appropriately formal style.			
Conventions			
• I use an ellipsis to omit irrelevant or redundant information and to highlight well-chosen evidence.			
• I use active and passive voice to emphasize either the actor or the action.			
• I maintain consistent verb mood.			
Writing Process			
• I complete all the steps in the End-of-Module Planning Packet.			
Total number of checks			

Volume of Reading Reflection Questions

The Great War, Grade 8, Module 2

Student Name:

Text:

Author:

Topic:

Genre/type of book:

Share your insights about your independent reading about World War I by responding to the questions below.

Informational Text

1. **Wonder:** What drew your attention to this text? What questions about World War I will this text address?

2. **Organize:** Summarize the author's presentation of information about World War I. How did this structure better help you understand different facets of the war?

3. **Reveal:** Select a specific word or phrase used to describe an event. How does the author's word choice indicate the tone of the text?

4. **Distill:** How does this text engage the reader and convey the impact of World War I on the soldiers who fought as well as the civilians at home?

5. **Know:** How does reading this text expand your knowledge and understanding of the events and the impact of World War I on both soldiers and civilians?

6. **Vocabulary:** Identify three to five vocabulary words presented in this text that are key to understanding the impact of World War I. Define each word and explain why it is an important word to know.

Literary Text

1. **Wonder:** What perspective on World War I did this text provide?

2. **Organize:** How did the author tell the story? What central themes emerged?

3. **Reveal:** How do specific language and structural choices of the author convey or develop a theme? What is the author's perspective on the war?

4. **Distill:** How do the challenges and experiences of the main characters in this work serve to illustrate the global impact of World War I?

Name _____

Date _____ Class _____

5. Know: In what ways has reading this text about World War I deepened your knowledge of, and understanding about, the impact of World War I on both soldiers and civilians?

6. Vocabulary: Identify three to five vocabulary words presented in this text that are key to understanding the impact of World War I on the main character.

WIT & WISDOM PARENT TIP SHEET

WHAT IS MY EIGHTH-GRADE STUDENT LEARNING IN MODULE 2?

Wit & Wisdom is our English curriculum. It builds knowledge of key topics in history, science, and literature through the study of excellent texts. By reading and responding to stories and nonfiction texts, we will build knowledge of the following topics:

Module 1: The Poetics and Power of Storytelling

Module 2: The Great War

Module 3: What Is Love?

Module 4: Teens as Change Agents

In this second module, *The Great War*, students will study how writers and artists tell the story of World War I.

OUR CLASS WILL READ THESE TEXTS:

Novel
- *All Quiet on the Western Front*, Erich Maria Remarque (translator A.W. Wheen)

Poetry
- "Dulce et Decorum Est," Wilfred Owen
- "In Flanders Fields," John McCrae

Articles
- "The Peace President Goes to War," Duane Damon
- "The War to End All Wars," Shari Lyn Zuber
- "The Teenage Soldiers of World War One," BBC Magazine
- "Fighting From the Trenches," Kathryn M. Horst
- "The Forgotten Female Shell-Shock Victims of World War I," Hannah Groch-Begley
- "'Your Country Needs You: Why Did So Many Volunteer in 1914?," Toby Thacker

OUR CLASS WILL EXAMINE THESE PAINTINGS:
- *Gassed*, John Singer Sargent
- *Soldiers Playing Cards*, Fernand Léger

OUR CLASS WILL WATCH THESE VIDEOS:

- Excerpts from *All Quiet on the Western Front*, Lewis Milestone:

    "The Charge"

    "Before the Storm"

    "Forgive me, Comrade"

OUR CLASS WILL ASK THESE QUESTIONS:

- Why did countries and individuals join World War I?
- How did the conditions on the front affect soldiers?
- How do texts inspired by World War I illuminate attitudes toward the war?
- What are the psychological effects of war?
- How does *All Quiet on the Western Front* illuminate the effects of World War I?

QUESTIONS TO ASK AT HOME:

As your eighth-grade student reads, ask:

- *What's happening?*
- *What does a closer look at words reveal about this text's deeper meaning?*

BOOKS TO READ AT HOME:

- *War Horse*, Michael Morpurgo
- *Private Peaceful*, Michael Morpurgo
- *The Family Romanov*, Candace Fleming
- *World War I: The Cause for War*, Natalie Hyde
- *The War to End All Wars*, Russell Freedman
- *The Guns of August*, Barbara Tuchman
- *The Yanks Are Coming*, Albert Marrin
- *Soldier Dog*, Sam Angus

IDEAS FOR DISCUSSING WORLD WAR I:

Watch a movie together that tells the story of World War I, such as Sergeant York. Ask:

- How did the filmmaker tell the story of World War I?
- How does this film compare to the novel you read in class?
- How does this film compare to the art you examined?

CREDITS

Great Minds® has made every effort to obtain permission for the reprinting of all copyrighted material. If any owner of copyrighted material is not acknowledged herein, please contact Great Minds® for proper acknowledgment in all future editions and reprints of this module.

- All material from the *Common Core State Standards for English Language Arts & Literacy in History/Social Studies, Science, and Technical Subjects* © Copyright 2010 National Governors Association Center for Best Practices and Council of Chief State School Officers. All rights reserved.

- All images are used under license from Shutterstock.com unless otherwise noted.

- Handouts 1A and 1C: "The War to End All Wars" by Shari Lyn Zuber from *Treaty of Versailles*, 1919, Cobblestone magazine, March 1998. Text copyright © 1998 by Carus Publishing Company. Reprinted by permission of Cricket Media. All Cricket Media material is copyrighted by Carus Publishing d/b/a Cricket Media, and/or various authors and illustrators. Any commercial use or distribution of material without permission is strictly prohibited. Please visit http://www.cricketmedia.com/info/licensing2 for licensing and http://www.cricketmedia.com for subscriptions

- Handout 1B: "The Peace President Goes to War" by Duane Damon from *US Involvement in World War I*, Cobblestone magazine, June 1986. Text copyright © 1986 by Carus Publishing Company. Reprinted by permission of Cricket Media. All Cricket Media material is copyrighted by Carus Publishing d/b/a Cricket Media, and/or various authors and illustrators. Any commercial use or distribution of material without permission is strictly prohibited. Please visit http://www.cricketmedia.com/info/licensing2 for licensing and http://www.cricketmedia.com for subscriptions

- Handout 12A: "Fighting From the Trenches" by Kathryn M. Horst from *US Involvement in World War I*, Cobblestone magazine, June 1986. Text copyright © 1986 by Carus Publishing Company. Reprinted by permission of Cricket Media. All Cricket Media material is copyrighted by Carus Publishing d/b/a Cricket Media, and/or various authors and illustrators. Any commercial use or distribution of material without permission is strictly prohibited. Please visit http://www.cricketmedia.com/info/licensing2 for licensing and http://www.cricketmedia.com for subscriptions

- For updated credit information, please visit http://witeng.link/credits.

ACKNOWLEDGMENTS

Great Minds® Staff

The following writers, editors, reviewers, and support staff contributed to the development of this curriculum.

Ann Brigham, Lauren Chapalee, Sara Clarke, Emily Climer, Lorraine Griffith, Emily Gula, Sarah Henchey, Trish Huerster, Stephanie Kane-Mainier, Lior Klirs, Liz Manolis, Andrea Minich, Lynne Munson, Marya Myers, Rachel Rooney, Aaron Schifrin, Danielle Shylit, Rachel Stack, Sarah Turnage, Michelle Warner, Amy Wierzbicki, Margaret Wilson, and Sarah Woodard.

Colleagues and Contributors

We are grateful for the many educators, writers, and subject-matter experts who made this program possible.

David Abel, Robin Agurkis, Elizabeth Bailey, Julianne Barto, Amy Benjamin, Andrew Biemiller, Charlotte Boucher, Sheila Byrd-Carmichael, Eric Carey, Jessica Carloni, Janine Cody, Rebecca Cohen, Elaine Collins, Tequila Cornelious, Beverly Davis, Matt Davis, Thomas Easterling, Jeanette Edelstein, Kristy Ellis, Moira Clarkin Evans, Charles Fischer, Marty Gephart, Kath Gibbs, Natalie Goldstein, Christina Gonzalez, Mamie Goodson, Nora Graham, Lindsay Griffith, Brenna Haffner, Joanna Hawkins, Elizabeth Haydel, Steve Hettleman, Cara Hoppe, Ashley Hymel, Carol Jago, Jennifer Johnson, Mason Judy, Gail Kearns, Shelly Knupp, Sarah Kushner, Shannon Last, Suzanne Lauchaire, Diana Leddy, David Liben, Farren Liben, Jennifer Marin, Susannah Maynard, Cathy McGath, Emily McKean, Jane Miller, Rebecca Moore, Cathy Newton, Turi Nilsson, Julie Norris, Galemarie Ola, Michelle Palmieri, Meredith Phillips, Shilpa Raman, Tonya Romayne, Emmet Rosenfeld, Jennifer Ruppel, Mike Russoniello, Deborah Samley, Casey Schultz, Renee Simpson, Rebecca Sklepovich, Amelia Swabb, Kim Taylor, Vicki Taylor, Melissa Thomson, Lindsay Tomlinson, Melissa Vail, Keenan Walsh, Julia Wasson, Lynn Welch, Yvonne Guerrero Welch, Emily Whyte, Lynn Woods, and Rachel Zindler.

Early Adopters

The following early adopters provided invaluable insight and guidance for Wit & Wisdom:

- Bourbonnais School District 53 • Bourbonnais, IL
- Coney Island Prep Middle School • Brooklyn, NY
- Gate City Charter School for the Arts • Merrimack, NH
- Hebrew Academy for Special Children • Brooklyn, NY
- Paris Independent Schools • Paris, KY
- Saydel Community School District • Saydel, IA
- Strive Collegiate Academy • Nashville, TN
- Valiente College Preparatory Charter School • South Gate, CA
- Voyageur Academy • Detroit, MI

Design Direction provided by Alton Creative, Inc.

Project management support, production design, and copyediting services provided by ScribeConcepts.com

Copyediting services provided by Fine Lines Editing

Product management support provided by Sandhill Consulting